Stories in the Stars

T0337792

Contents

Written by Anita Ganeri

Illustrated by Linh Nguyen

Collins

1 The sky

When you look up at the sky, what do you see?
In the day, you can see the Sun. At night, you can see
the Moon and stars. Today, we know a lot about
the Sun, Moon and stars.

But long ago, people didn't understand what they were. Before science was able to explain what we know today, people made sense of the world with stories and fables. These stories helped them to understand the world they lived in. Do you know any myths or legends about the Sun, Moon and stars?

Look for any similarities and differences between the stories in this book.

2 The Sun

Over the course of history, people have feared and worshipped the Sun. Even without the science we have today, our **ancestors** knew how important the Sun was to life on Earth. Without the Sun's light, plants could not grow, animals that eat plants would have nothing to eat, and so the food chains we rely on could not exist.

The Sun is a star. It is a hot, spinning ball of glowing gas, and it gives Earth heat and light. Temperatures inside the Sun can reach 15 million degrees **Celsius**! Luckily, we are far enough away to not get too hot – the Sun is about 150 million kilometres away from Earth.

The Sun is made up mainly of two gases: hydrogen and helium.

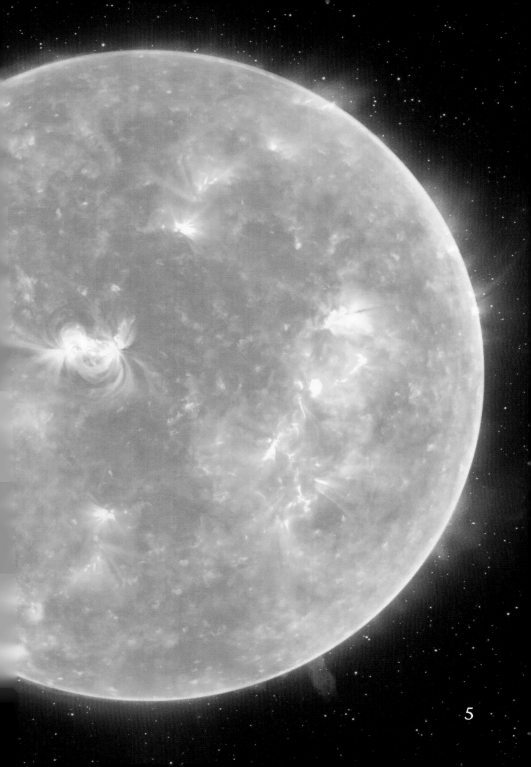

It takes Earth a year (365 days) to go around the Sun once.

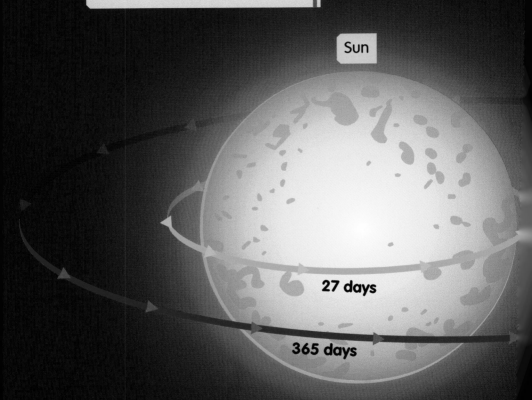

Sun

27 days

365 days

We know these facts about the Sun because of discoveries in science. Before these discoveries, different cultures around the world created their own stories to explain the Sun.

Let's take a look at some of these stories. Think about what the stories tell us about the Sun and the cultures the stories come from. Are there any similarities between the stories?

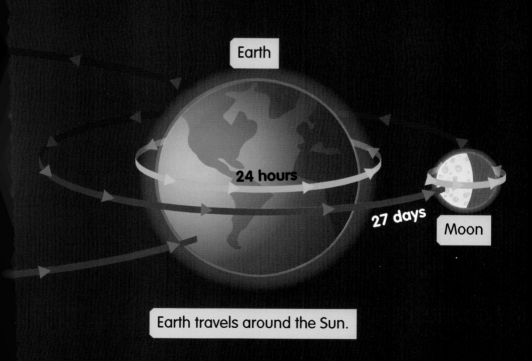

Earth

24 hours

27 days

Moon

Earth travels around the Sun.

Chariot of the Sun

The Norse people had their own **theories** about the Sun, Moon and stars being made from sparks of fire. Legend states that the gods gave the Sun and Moon two chariots to ride in. By day, the Sun's chariot raced across the sky. By night, it was the Moon's turn.

Fact File

Culture: *Norse*

Place: *Northern Europe*

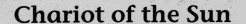

A giant called Mundilfari lived on Earth and had two children – he named the girl Sol, after the Sun, and the boy Mani, after the Moon. This angered the gods and they thought Mundilfari should be punished for using gods' names. The gods sent Sol away from home and put her in the sky to drive the Sun's chariot.

Every day, Sol drove the chariot across the sky. As she drove, she held up a giant shield that stopped Earth from being burnt by the Sun's fierce heat. Sol didn't dare to slow down, as an evil wolf raced after the chariot. If it got near enough to bite her, the Sun would go out.

How does this myth help to explain the relationship between the Sun and Earth? It shows how much understanding Norse people had about the Sun's power and its fierce heat. Today, we know that the ozone layer protects Earth from the Sun's harmful rays.

When the Sun went out

This Japanese myth talks of Susanoo, the storm god, and his sister, Amaterasu, the goddess of the Sun.

One day, during an argument, Susanoo picked up his horse, and threw it into Amaterasu's hall.

Fact File

Culture: Ancient Japan

Place: Japan

Amaterasu was so frightened, she hid in a cave and the Sun went out. The whole world was plunged into darkness. Crops couldn't grow and people went hungry.

The gods had to act quickly. Omoikane, the god of **wisdom** and intelligence, had a plan. He planted a tree outside the cave and hung a long rope of jewels from it.

The goddess of the dawn danced while the other gods cheered. Inside the cave, Amaterasu heard them and peered out of the cave for a better look. Omoikane grabbed her and held her tight. The other gods stretched the rope jewels across the cave to stop her going back in. And so, the Sun shone once again on the world.

Did you know?

Japanese people call their country "Nippon". This means "Land of the Rising Sun". The flag of Japan shows a round, red sun. The emperor of Japan is said to be the **descendant** of the Sun goddess Amaterasu.

Which was your favourite story?
What were the common themes?
What qualities did the Sun goddess have in both myths?

3 The Moon

Scientists have been studying the Moon for years. It is Earth's closest neighbour and it is almost 385,000 kilometres away. However, before scientists worked out how to study the Moon, people used to tell stories to explain how the Moon came to be.

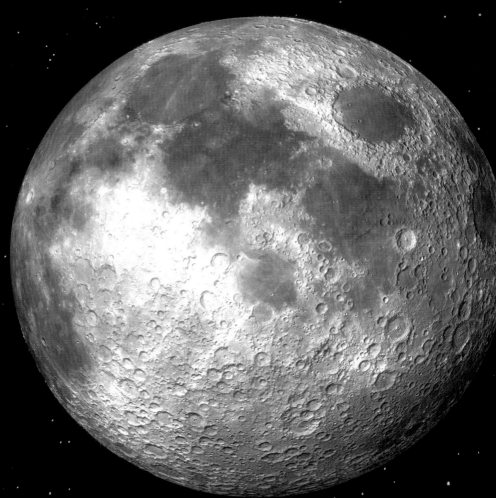

The Moon is the second brightest object in the sky after the Sun. It looks bright in the night sky because it reflects light from the Sun. The Moon was formed 4.6 billion years ago, but it took until 1969 for humans to land on the Moon for the first time.

Astronaut Buzz Aldrin walks on the Moon.

The Moon is just over a quarter the size of Earth.
It travels once around Earth every 27 days.

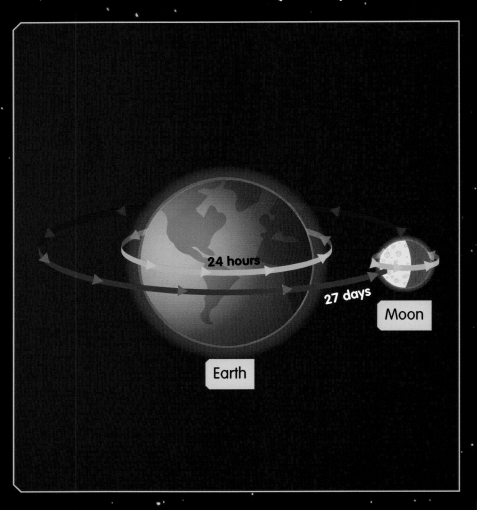

24 hours

27 days

Moon

Earth

The Moon's surface has huge craters. There are also
big, dark patches, called seas. From Earth, the craters
and seas look like shapes.

All around the world, there are many myths about the Moon's creation, and stories to explain the "face" that some people can see in it.

Have you ever seen a face on the Moon? How do you think it would feel to walk on the Moon?

Lady in the Moon

This Chinese myth tells of Chang'e and her husband, Hou Yi. He was a great **archer**.

Fact File

Culture: Ancient China

Place: China

At that time, there were ten suns that shone one by one. But, one day, all of them shone at once and the heat was unbearable.

The emperor ordered Hou Yi to shoot the suns down, so only one sun was left. As a thank you, Hou Yi was given a magic potion that allowed the person who drank it to live forever. There was only enough for one person, so he hid the potion away.

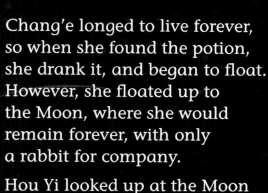

Chang'e longed to live forever, so when she found the potion, she drank it, and began to float. However, she floated up to the Moon, where she would remain forever, with only a rabbit for company.

Hou Yi looked up at the Moon every night and longed to be with his wife again.

In China, people see the shapes of Chang'e and her rabbit in the Moon at night and they celebrate the Lady in the Moon every year at the Moon Festival. It is the second most important festival in China after the Chinese New Year celebrations.

What do you think about what Chang'e did?

Rabbit in the Moon

The Aztecs believed that a terrible flood had wiped out the world. Although the gods made a new sky, there was still no Sun or Moon, so Earth was dark and cold for many years.

Fact File

Culture: Aztecs

Place: Central Mexico

The gods needed two gods to become the new Sun and Moon. Two gods stepped forward – one was boastful and the other brave.

In order to become the Sun, they had to jump into a blazing fire. The boastful god ran towards the fire, but at the last minute, he was too scared to jump in. The brave god didn't hesitate and ran towards the fire. He jumped straight into the flames and became the new Sun! The boastful god hated losing, so he jumped into the fire behind the brave god.

The next day, the brave god rose into the sky as the new Sun and the boastful god appeared as the new Moon. He wanted to shine as brightly as the Sun, but the gods did not allow it. One god picked up a rabbit and threw it up to the Moon to cover its surface, so that it was not so bright. It left a mark that looked like the Moon was bruised.

Did you know?

The Aztecs saw the shape of a rabbit in the Moon. The Chinese saw a woman and rabbit. In Europe, many people saw the face of the "man in the Moon".

What do you see when you look at the Moon? What are the similarities and differences between these Moon stories?

4 The stars

Stars look like tiny dots of light in the night sky, but they are actually giant balls of very hot gas. There are billions of stars. They vary in size from about ten times smaller than the Sun to about 2,000 times bigger than the Sun in **diameter**.

Many **constellations** are named after characters in ancient mythology, or animals. Depending on where you live on Earth, you can see different constellations.

The Big Dipper is part of the Great Bear constellation and is mainly visible in the **Northern Hemisphere**.

The Southern Cross is only visible in the **Southern Hemisphere**.

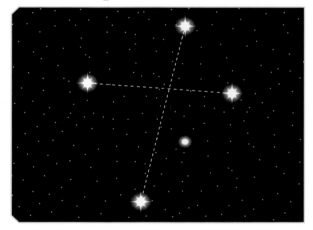

Long ago, people came up with their own stories to explain the different patterns of stars. What patterns have you spotted?

Orion the Hunter

Orion is one of the best-known constellations. The Ancient Greeks named it after Orion, the son of the sea god, Poseidon. Orion was tall, strong and brave, and a great hunter.

Artemis, the goddess of the Moon, fell madly in love with Orion and wanted to marry him. But her twin brother, Apollo, hated Orion. To stop his sister marrying Orion, Apollo plotted to kill him.

Fact File

Culture: Ancient Greek

Place: Greece

Apollo tricked his sister into killing Orion while he swam in the sea. She was heartbroken. To honour him, she placed Orion among the stars as a hunter, where he could shine forever.

Did you know?

Orion is easy to spot in the night sky. A very bright star marks his right shoulder. A line of three stars make up his belt.

Osiris and the pharaoh's soul

In Ancient Egypt, the Orion constellation was known as Osiris, the god of the dead.

Long ago, Osiris ruled Egypt for many years. His brother, Seth, was jealous of his power and wanted to kill Osiris. He held a feast in the palace to say thank you to Osiris. At the feast, there was fine food to eat, and singing, dancing and party games.

Fact File

Culture: Ancient Egyptian

Place: Egypt

At the end of the party, Seth tricked Osiris into getting into a chest, and he threw it into the River Nile.

His queen, Isis, searched for the chest until, one day, she found it on the shore. She carried it home and used her magical powers to bring Osiris back to life.

Osiris could not stay on Earth, so he was made god of the dead. His soul flew up into the sky to be among the stars. So, the constellation the Greeks saw as Orion was known as Osiris to the Egyptians.

What similarities do these myths have?

The Southern Cross – Giraffe becomes a star

The Southern Cross is another constellation that has many stories about it.

The San peoples in South Africa tell the story of all the animals on Earth having a job to do, except for Giraffe.

Giraffe wanted to be useful like the other animals, so one day, the animals had a good idea. As the Sun often got lost on its journey across the sky, it needed someone to guide it.

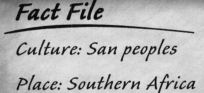

Fact File

Culture: San peoples

Place: Southern Africa

Giraffe was so tall that he could poke his head above the trees and help the Sun.

Whenever the Sun went the wrong way, Giraffe stretched his long neck and nudged it back into place. To thank him, some of the stars moved so that they always pointed at the Sun. The local people called this constellation "Giraffe".

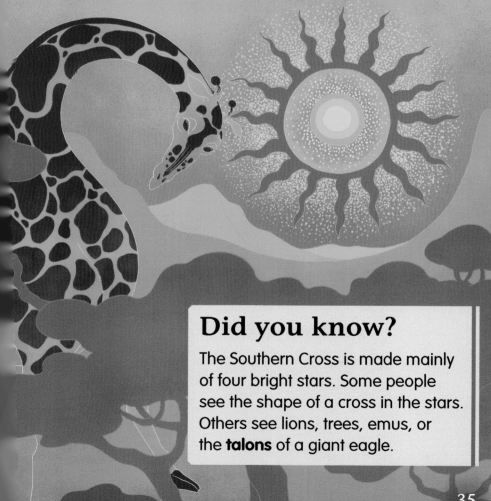

Did you know?

The Southern Cross is made mainly of four bright stars. Some people see the shape of a cross in the stars. Others see lions, trees, emus, or the **talons** of a giant eagle.

The Southern Cross

According to some First Nation
Australians, if you can spot
a dark patch between the stars,
this is the head of a large bird
called an emu. It was believed
that this Emu once lived on
Earth and a gust of wind blew
Emu into the sky.

Fact File

Culture: First
Nation Australians

Place: Australia

Emu wandered across the sky until she found
the camp of the stars and asked them if she could live
with them. They said yes, but they asked Emu to help
them to hold up the sky.

In return for her help, the stars shuffled about in
the sky to make room for her and created the Southern
Cross in the process.

Coyote scatters the stars

The Navajo Nation is the largest Native American tribe in the USA. They believe that when Earth was new, there was no Sun or Moon. The gods painted the Sun and the Moon on the skies, but the night sky still looked empty and dark.

Fact File

Culture: The
Navajo Nation

Place: USA

The fire god stamped his feet, and sparkling stars burst up all around him. He made constellations of stars from crystals so it wasn't dark anymore.

A coyote appeared and grabbed the crystals, and blew them all over the sky. While the fire god's star patterns stayed where they were, all around, stars fell in a jumble. This explained why they could see clear patterns of stars, surrounded by lots of stars that didn't make a pattern.

The great canoe of stars

This Maori myth has a different theory. Tama-rereti was a brave warrior who went fishing in the lake. After catching lots of fish, Tama-rereti fell asleep in his canoe.

His canoe drifted all the way to the other end of the lake. He woke up a long way from home and it was getting dark. He pulled his canoe onto a nearby beach, lit a fire and cooked some fish.

Fact File

Culture: Maori

Place: New Zealand

As night was falling fast, Tama-rereti loaded his canoe with shiny pebbles and sailed his canoe up to the great river in the sky, throwing the pebbles as he went.

They became stars so he could see well enough to find his way home before dawn.

To thank Tama-rereti, the gods put his canoe among the stars where it sails, forever, through the night.

Did you know?

The "river in the sky" from this story is what we call the Milky Way. It looks like a long, white streak in the night sky. The Milky Way is a galaxy – an enormous group of stars, which includes our Sun.

5 Conclusion

You have read some scientific facts about the Sun, Moon and stars. You have also read some fascinating stories from the past of how people used to explain the world they lived in.

What do you think about these myths and legends?

Which ones have the biggest overlap with the science we know today?

Glossary

ancestors people from your distant past who you are related to

archer a person who shoots with a bow and arrow

Celsius a temperature scale

constellations groups of stars in a pattern

descendant a person who is related to a particular ancestor from the past

diameter the width of a circle or sphere/ball

Northern Hemisphere the half of Earth that is above the equator/middle

Southern Hemisphere the half of Earth that is below the equator/middle

talons claws

theories ideas that explain something

wisdom the quality of having experience, knowledge and making good decisions

Index

Starry stories around the world

Retell the stories from each country.

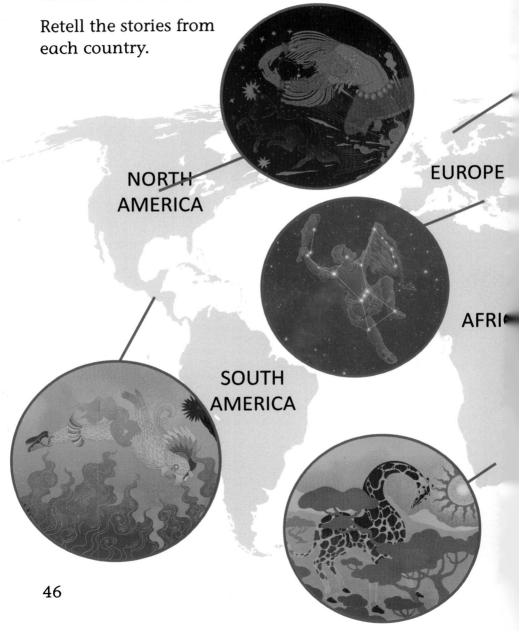

NORTH AMERICA

EUROPE

SOUTH AMERICA

AFRIC

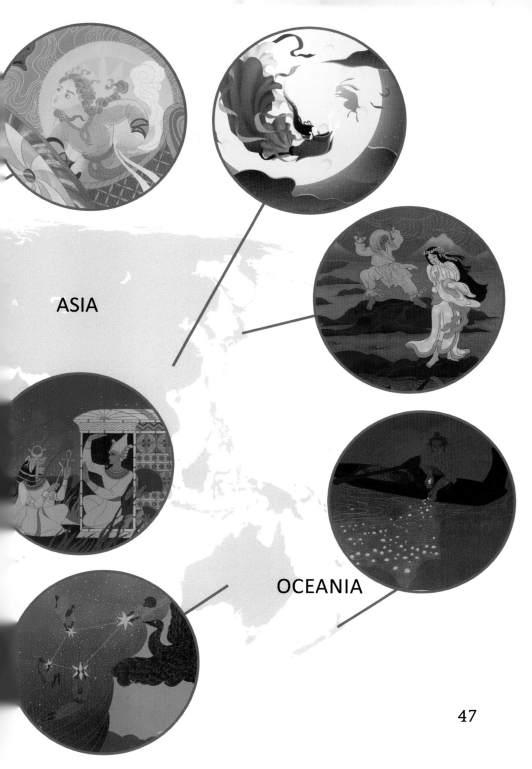

ASIA

OCEANIA

Ideas for reading

Written by Christine Whitney
Primary Literacy Consultant

Reading objectives:
- be introduced to non-fiction books that are structured in different ways
- listen to, discuss and express views about non-fiction
- retrieve and record information from non-fiction
- discuss and clarify the meanings of words

Spoken language objectives:
- participate in discussion
- speculate, hypothesise, imagine and explore ideas through talk
- ask relevant questions

Curriculum links: History: Develop an awareness of the past; Writing: Write for different purposes

Word count: 2655

Interest words: fables, theories, constellation, hemisphere

Resources: paper, pencils and crayons, access to the internet

Build a context for reading
- Play 5 in 3! Ask the group to name five facts about the Sun, Moon and stars in three minutes.
- Show the title of the book. Ask the group to share any stories or rhymes they know about the Sun, Moon or stars.
- Together, read the blurb on the back cover of the book. Ask children to predict what stories might have been told in the past to explain the presence of the Sun, Moon and stars.

Understand and apply reading strategies
- Read Chapters 1 and 2 together. Ask children to summarise the facts, not stories or fables, about the Sun.
- In the Norse stories, Sol *held up a giant shield that stopped Earth from being burnt by the Sun's fierce heat*. Ask children to name the layer which we now know protects *Earth from the Sun's harmful rays*.